EDGE
BOOKS

DIRT BIKES

Motocross
Freestyle

by Tina P. Schwartz

Capstone
press

Mankato, Minnesota

Edge Books are published by Capstone Press
151 Good Counsel Drive, P.O. Box 669, Mankato, Minnesota 56002
www.capstonepress.com

Library of Congress Cataloging-in-Publication Data
Schwartz, Tina P.
    Motocross freestyle / by Tina P. Schwartz.
    p. cm.—(Edge books. Dirt bikes)
    Includes bibliographical references and index.
    Summary: Describes the sport of freestyle motocross, including the major
competitions, stunts, and athletes involved.
    ISBN 0-7368-2436-7 (hardcover)
    1. Motocross—Juvenile literature. [1. Motocross. 2. Motorcycle racing.] I. Title.
II. Series.
GV1060.12.S44 2004
796.7'56—dc22   2003013715

Editorial Credits
Angela Kaelberer, editor; Molly Nei, series designer; Jason Knudson, book designer;
    Jo Miller, photo researcher

Photo Credits
Anthony Scavo, 6, 9
Artemis Images/Ron McQueeney, 18, 19
Corbis/AFP, 26; Duomo, 25; Luca Babini, 12; Reuters NewMedia Inc., 5
Getty Images/Donald Miralle, 27; Elsa, 14–15, 20–21, 29
SportsChrome-USA/Rob Tringali Jr., cover, 10, 11, 16
The News Journal/Robert Craig, 22

**Capstone Press thanks Jason Huggler, promotion manager of the International
Freestyle Motocross Association, for his assistance with this book.**

1 2 3 4 5 6 09 08 07 06 05 04

Table of Contents

CHAPTER I

Freestyle Motocross

On August 16, 2002, freestyle motocross rider Mike Metzger took his last run at the X Games in Philadelphia, Pennsylvania. He landed trick after trick, including a rock solid and a heart attack.

Metzger planned to end his run with an even more extreme trick, the backflip. Just two weeks earlier, Travis Pastrana and Metzger had become the first riders to ever land the trick in competition. They both performed backflips at the Gravity Games in Cleveland, Ohio.

Learn about:
- The backflip
- A new sport
- Tricks

Mike Metzger wanted to land the first backflip at the X Games.

The kiss of death is one of the most extreme freestyle tricks.

Metzger rode his bike up the ramp. As he flipped the bike, he was 40 feet (12 meters) above the ramp. Metzger cleared the 46-foot (14-meter) jump for a perfect landing. But he was not finished. He sped up and flipped the bike across an 80-foot (24-meter) jump. Again, he landed perfectly. Metzger's two backflips earned him a gold medal.

Freestyle Motocross

During the 1990s, some motocross racers started doing tricks at the end of races or between races. Soon, riders held contests to see who could do the best tricks. In 1998, the International Freestyle Motocross Association (IFMA) formed to set up rules for the sport.

During early competitions, people were amazed to see no-footers, no-handers, and other basic tricks. Today, riders do more extreme tricks, such as the kiss of death and the cliffhanger. Each year, riders invent new tricks that are even more difficult and daring.

CHAPTER 2

Equipment and Safety

Freestyle bikes are much like bikes used in motocross racing, but there are some important differences. Freestyle riders land hard after tricks. Freestyle bikes' shock absorbers are strong enough to cushion the rider's landing. The bikes also have reinforced handlebars. These strong handlebars support the weight of riders as they do tricks such as the dead body or the heel clicker.

Learn about:
- Bikes
- Skills
- Equipment

Sturdy handlebars support the rider during a dead body.

Riders use grips in the bike's seat to do Superman seat grabs.

Freestyle riders cut holes into the number plates on either side of their bikes. These holes are called grips or grab holes. Riders hang onto the grips to perform the heart attack and other tricks. Some riders also cut grips into the seat. They use seat grips to do Superman seat grabs and rock solids.

Training

Training is important for freestyle riders. The top riders practice many hours each day. Most freestyle riders use BMX bicycles to train.

They practice stunts on these bikes before trying to do the tricks on their motorcycles.

Riders also make sure their bodies are in top shape. They eat healthy food, get plenty of exercise, and lift weights.

Top freestyle riders practice many hours each day.

Full-face helmets and goggles help protect riders.

Gear

Motocross riders wear safety gear both in practice and in competitions. A full-face helmet is the most important piece of safety equipment. Goggles protect riders' eyes. Riders wear hard plastic body armor to protect their upper bodies. Some riders also wear a belt that protects their kidneys and spine.

Riders' clothing also helps them stay safe. They wear padded pants and long-sleeved vented jerseys. The vented material lets air through to keep riders' skin cool. Riders wear high, steel-toed boots to protect their feet, ankles, and shins. Padded leather gloves protect riders' hands.

CHAPTER 3

Competitions and Tricks

The freestyle motocross season runs from January to March, and then again from August to December. The IFMA hosts at least 35 events each year, including the Vans Triple Crown. These three races are held in April, October, and November. Freestyle riders also compete in the X Games and the Gravity Games.

Learn about:
- Events
- Judging
- Tricks

Freestyle riders compete in the X Games each year.

Classes and Sponsors

Riders compete either as amateurs or professionals. Both amateur and pro riders compete for prize money, but pro riders usually compete more often. Pro riders earn a

Riders have logos from sponsoring companies on their bikes and clothing.

living from the sport. Amateur riders may still be in school or have another job.

Both amateur and pro riders can have sponsors. These companies give money and equipment to riders. In return, the riders show the company's logos on their bikes and clothing. They also may appear in advertisements for the company.

Scoring

At competitions, each rider makes up a 1- to 2-minute program of tricks. Riders are judged on how well they perform the tricks. The judges often give higher scores for more difficult tricks. Judges also score riders on originality, such as doing a new version of a basic trick.

In IFMA events, two to three judges score each event. Each rider can receive 100 points from each judge. All the judges' scores are then averaged to make up a rider's final score. The rider with the most points at the end of a competition wins.

During a nothing, the rider lifts both hands and feet off the bike.

Basic Tricks

Riders use their hands and feet to perform some of the simplest tricks. They take their hands off the handlebars to do a no-hander. They take their feet off the footpegs for a no-footer. The trick is called a nothing if the rider lifts both hands and feet.

A can-can is another basic trick. During a can-can, the rider swings one leg over the seat, so both legs are on the same side of the bike. The rider then stretches one leg out from the bike while leaving the other foot on the footpeg. For a no-footed can-can, the rider stretches both feet out from the bike.

Many riders perform whips and heel clickers. For a whip, the rider twists the bike during the highest point of the jump so the bike lies as flat as possible. During a heel clicker, the rider keeps the hands on the handlebars while bringing the feet up around the arms. The rider then clicks the heels together above the front fender.

A rider stretches both legs over the bike during a no-footed can-can.

With experience, riders move on to more difficult tricks. To do a Saran Wrap, a rider puts both hands on the grips. The rider stretches one leg between the arms. The rider then lifts one arm while swinging the leg around the handlebars and back on the footpeg. For a cliffhanger, a rider hooks the feet under the handlebars. The rider then stretches back over the bike while raising the arms over the head. To do a Superman seat grab, a rider grabs the bike's seat while kicking the legs back behind the bike.

The rock solid is one of the most difficult tricks. The trick begins like a Superman seat grab. Then, the rider lets go of the bike for a few seconds. No part of the rider touches the bike. The rider finishes the trick by grabbing the seat and getting back on the bike.

The rider completely lets go of the bike during a rock solid.

Heidi Henry took part in an exhibition event at the 2002 X Games.

Women In Freestyle

Until recently, all of the top freestyle riders have been men. In 2002, the X Games added an exhibition event for female riders.

Heidi Henry and Heather Williams showed off their style at the 2002 X Games. Henry raced motocross bikes for several years before trying freestyle in 2002. Williams is a wakeboarder who started riding freestyle just one month before the X Games.

Freestyle is not yet a popular sport for women riders. In 2003, no female riders took part in the X Games.

CHAPTER 4

Freestyle Greats

Many of the first freestyle riders still compete today. The sport also attracts many young riders.

Mike Jones

Mike Jones is one of the oldest and most daring freestyle riders. Jones was born in Pennsylvania in 1966. He started riding at age 6.

Jones invented the kiss of death. For this trick, Jones throws his bike into a vertical position. He does a handstand while holding the handlebars and bending to touch the front fender with his helmet.

Learn about:
- The first freestylers
- Today's greats
- Rising stars

Mike Jones helped start the sport of freestyle motocross.

Travis Pastrana competes in both freestyle and racing.

Travis Pastrana

Many people consider Travis Pastrana today's best freestyle rider. Pastrana began riding at age 3 and won his first X Games gold medal in 1999 at age 15. Pastrana won the freestyle gold medal again in 2000, 2001, and 2003. He also won the Gravity Games freestyle gold medal in 2001 and 2002.

In 2003, Pastrana lost a major competition for the first time. Nate Adams defeated him for the Gravity Games gold medal.

The Godfather

Mike Metzger was born in 1975 in California. People call him the "godfather of freestyle" because he made up many basic and extreme freestyle tricks. He is known for the Saran Wrap, the Superman, the heel clicker, and the backflip.

Mike Metzger did this backflip at the 2003 Winter X Games.

At the 2002 X Games, Metzger's two backflips in a row earned him a gold medal. He called the trick the Double Fritz after his grandfather, Fritz Metzger.

New Stars

Each year, riders move up from the amateur to the pro ranks. These riders bring new tricks and ideas to the sport.

Drake McElroy started riding in 1983 at age 2. Today, he is known for a trick called the dead body or the corpse. To do this trick, McElroy grabs the handlebars and stretches his legs out in front of his bike. He then lays his body flat above the bike.

Nate Adams was born in 1984 in Arizona. He started riding at age 8. In April 2003, he did the first backflip no-hander lander in competition. Five months later, he won the gold medal in freestyle at the Gravity Games. At that event, he became the first rider to defeat Travis Pastrana in a major competition.

Freestyle riders combine their creativity with their love of racing. These riders will continue to test the limits of what a rider and a bike can do.

The dead body is Drake McElroy's most famous trick.

Glossary

amateur (AM-uh-chur)—an athlete who usually does not earn a living from competing in a sport

body armor (BOD-ee AR-mur)—a plastic shield with foam lining that motocross riders usually wear under their clothing

goggles (GOG-uhlz)—glasses worn by motocross riders to protect their eyes

professional (pruh-FESH-uh-nuhl)—an athlete who earns a living from competing in a sport

shock absorber (SHAWK ab-SORB-uhr)—a part that lessens the impact to the bike from bumps and rough roads

sponsor (SPON-sur)—a company that helps pay an athlete's expenses; in return, athletes use and help advertise the sponsor's products.

Read More

Blomquist, Christopher. *Motocross in the X Games.* A Kid's Guide to the X Games. New York: PowerKids Press, 2003.

Coombs, Davey. *American Motocross Illustrated.* Morgan Hill, Calif.: Fox Racing, 2002.

Schaefer, A. R. *Extreme Freestyle Motocross Moves.* Behind the Moves. Mankato, Minn.: Capstone Press, 2003.

Useful Addresses

American Motorcyclist Association
13515 Yarmouth Drive
Pickerington, OH 43147-8273

International Freestyle Motocross Association
2501 Parkway Drive, Suite 105
Fort Worth, TX 76102

Internet Sites

FactHound offers a safe, fun way to find Internet sites related to this book. All of the sites on FactHound have been researched by our staff.

Here's how:

1. Visit *www.facthound.com*
2. Type in this special code **0736824367** for age-appropriate sites. Or enter a search word related to this book for a more general search.
3. Click on the **Fetch It** button.

FactHound will fetch the best sites for you!

Index